GIG JOBS IN
GAMING

by Clara MacCarald

BrightP◊int Press

San Diego, CA

BrightP◇int Press

© 2023 BrightPoint Press
an imprint of ReferencePoint Press, Inc.
Printed in the United States

For more information, contact:
BrightPoint Press
PO Box 27779
San Diego, CA 92198

www.BrightPointPress.com

LIBRARY OF CONGRESS CATALOGING-IN-PUBLICATION DATA

Names: MacCarald, Clara, 1979- author.
Title: Gig jobs in gaming / by Clara MacCarald.
Description: San Diego, CA: BrightPoint, 2023. | Series: Exploring jobs in
   the gig economy | Includes bibliographical references and index. |
   Audience: Grades 10-12
Identifiers: LCCN 2022007172 (print) | LCCN 2022007173 (eBook) | ISBN
   9781678203863 (hardcover) | ISBN 9781678203870 (eBook)
Subjects: LCSH: Video gamers--Vocational guidance--Juvenile literature. |
   Video games industry--Juvenile literature. | Gig economy--Juvenile
   literature.
Classification: LCC GV1469.3 .M327 2023 (print) | LCC GV1469.3 (eBook) |
   DDC 794.8092--dc23/eng/20220316
LC record available at https://lccn.loc.gov/2022007172
LC eBook record available at https://lccn.loc.gov/2022007173

CONTENTS

AT A GLANCE

- Gig workers don't work a long-term job for a single company. They work independently and can take on single projects or short-term positions.

- The internet gave gig workers new ways to make money, whether through selling games more widely or by streaming their gameplay.

- Independent game developers can make their own games, or people can take gigs to work on other people's games. A gig worker might write code, record sounds, or do anything else that's required.

- Gaming journalists write pieces for blogs, magazines, and websites. They might write about a person, a game, or any other part of the gaming business.

- Game streamers record themselves playing games, often while talking and chatting with viewers. Streamers make money from subscribers, ads, and sponsors.

- Working a gig job in gaming can be hard. Lots of people are competing for work, the pay can be low, and gig jobs lack certain benefits that regular jobs offer.

- Game streaming has become widely popular, especially after the COVID-19 pandemic led to more people being stuck at home.

- The future of gig work will be affected by new laws that try to decide who is a gig worker, as well as the responses of companies and workers to those laws.

STREAMING A RECORD

Niftski moved his fingers over the keyboard. Niftski wasn't the man's real name. It was his streaming username. On a screen, the character Mario hopped over pipes. While Niftski played *Super Mario Bros.*, he said, "I know I can get this. It's just a matter of time."[1] His goal was to beat a speed record for the game.

Many gamers try to complete games as quickly as possible. This is called speedrunning.

Niftski is a streamer. He plays games and streams them live online. Fans can communicate with him or each other. A camera shows his hands on the keyboard.

Super Mario Bros. was first released in 1985. Since then, many other video games, toys, and movies have come out starring Mario.

The seconds ticked away. Mario avoided

enemy mushrooms, called Goombas, and

dashed into a castle. Niftski thanked a new

follower while keeping his attention on the game. Streamers earn money when people **subscribe** to their channel.

Niftski's hands moved smoothly. The sounds of the video game mixed with his tapping on the keyboard. Every jump Mario made was perfect. He hopped over turtles, or Koopas. He leaped to pick up coins. The chat sped up as viewers began to get excited. He was on pace for a new record. Niftski told himself to stay calm.

The game got harder. Mario jumped over lava pits and dodged fireballs. Niftski just kept going. Messages zipped by in the chat.

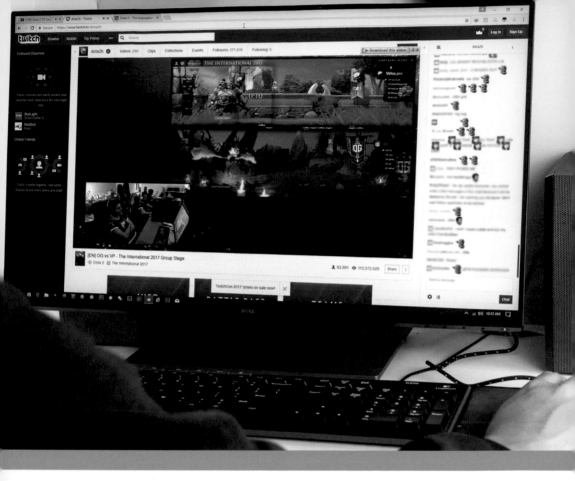

Some streaming websites, such as Twitch, allow viewers to chat with the person streaming.

Mario hopped over his final enemy. He arrived at the princess with four minutes and fifty-four seconds on the clock. It was a new record.

Niftski shouted happily. The chat exploded with excitement. His fans congratulated him.

WORKING THE GAME

Niftski is a **gig** worker. Gig workers are people who don't work a regular job with a steady income. Workers may work a short-term position as a gig, doing almost everything a long-term worker would do. Others take on gigs that are each a single project. For example, a **freelancer** can work gigs for several different clients at once.

Gaming has many opportunities for gig work. In 2021, the gaming business around the world was worth more than $300 billion. Lots of people enjoy gaming and want to make money from it. However, finding success as a gig worker in gaming takes hard work.

Streaming is a popular gig job. As of December 2021, Twitch alone had 7.6 million streamers.

CHAPTER ONE

THE HISTORY OF GIG JOBS IN GAMING

Computer games are almost as old as computers themselves. People made the first games to test the machines or to have fun. Over time, gaming became a business. Companies began creating games. More and more video game studios opened, leading to even more games.

Video games can be played on many different devices. Computers, gaming consoles, and even cell phones can run video games.

As video games spread, gamers found new ways to work. People could write code for games on home computers and sell them. Gaming magazines gave writers places to sell articles. The 2000s and

2010s saw the rise of video sharing over the internet. Gamers could make money at home playing the games they loved.

THE BIRTH OF GAMING

Early electronic computers date back to the 1940s. The machines were huge. They could occupy a whole room. Regular people couldn't buy computers. To see one of the machines, a person would have to go to a lab or to a university.

Scientists wanted to test all the things computers could do. One method was by creating games. One of the earliest was *Spacewar!* Two players each controlled

One of the first electronic computers was built in the 1940s. It was designed to help the United States fight in World War II (1939–1945).

their own spaceship. The ships fired at each

other. Students first made the program as

an experiment. The **developers** passed the

code to students who used computers at other universities.

Many people worked on *Spacewar!* to add challenges for players. These independent developers worked for fun, not for money. Independent developers don't belong to a big company. Their products are often called indie games for short.

The prize for the winner of the first ever video game contest in 1972 was a magazine subscription. The winner would also have his or her photo appear in an article in the magazine. The article itself was an early example of gaming journalism.

Even in those early days, people realized

the players were putting on a show that

viewers could enjoy. Stewart Brand, who

organized the contest, pointed out the

appeal. He said, "Five players sitting next

to each other yelling and banging away on

SPACEWAR!

Spacewar! started as a simple battle. The ships moved, but the stars didn't. But every developer who worked on the game made things more interesting. One made the background the real night sky. Another developer gave gravity to the central star. Players could get sucked in if they weren't careful. And then the ships could run out of fuel. *Spacewar!* opened people's minds to the many things a computer game could do.

their buttons added a nice sort of physical violence to the onscreen violence that was going on."[2]

Also in 1972, the electronic tennis game *Pong* arrived in arcades. Arcades are places where visitors play coin-operated games. A few years later, a home version of *Pong* became available. *Pong* was the first video game to be a huge success.

A POPULAR PASTIME

Arcades spread. People bought consoles so they could play their favorite games at home. A growing number of homes also had personal computers. Along with

Arcade games reached the peak of their popularity in the 1970s and 1980s. However, some arcades can still be found today.

games came more opportunities for

gaming journalism.

Arnie Katz, Bill Kunkel, and Joyce

Worley were early players and writers. In

1981, they started a new magazine called

Electronic Games. The team worked as freelancers on the first issue. The magazine covered nothing but video games. It was the first to do so, but others soon followed.

In 1983, the market for consoles crashed. Lots of gamers turned to computers instead. Developers could publish their code in magazines for other gamers to use. They could also sell copies through the mail. Soon, though, large game companies took control of the market. It became a lot harder to work as an indie developer rather than as part of a big company.

GAMING MOVES ONLINE

The beginnings of the internet date back to the 1960s. But internet access did not become common for everyday people until the 1990s. Over time, indie developers were able to reach out to more customers

THE WORST GAME EVER MADE

The main cause of the 1983 video game crash was too many consoles on the market and not enough good games. But many blamed the crash on a game called *E.T.* The game was based on the 1982 movie of the same name. It had an alien named E.T. looking for bits of a telephone. The quality of the play was terrible. The character kept getting stuck in traps. Some people called it the worst game ever made. Millions of copies went unsold.

through the internet. In 2003, the game company Valve created a service called Steam. For a few years Valve sold only its own products on Steam. In 2005, it allowed other companies to sell their games on the **platform**. Steam became a new way for developers to reach gamers.

Gamers had been posting videos of their gameplay to a website called Machinima since 2000. In 2005, the video-sharing website YouTube started. It offered a free and easy way to post videos online. Gaming video content became more popular. In 2011, a new service called Twitch started

As of 2021, Steam was one of the most popular places to buy computer games.

operating. Twitch is an internet platform for

streamers. From the beginning, Twitch was

all about gaming.

Indie developers hadn't gone away.

However, they had few chances to make it

big. Game developer Rami Ismail said, "If

you look back in 2008 when indie games

were starting to gain ground, it was this

underground thing."[3] Lots of gamers weren't aware of them.

In 2008, indie games caught people's attention with the release of popular titles such as *Braid*. Users could download *Braid* on the Xbox 360 console. The game was a quest for a princess with some twists. Developer Jonathan Blow created 38 levels with puzzles to solve and foes to face. Players who got into trouble could go back in time. And at the end, the player discovered the princess didn't want to be rescued. *Braid* delighted the industry. Blow made millions of dollars.

Minecraft was released as an indie game in 2009. It was later bought by Microsoft in 2014.

Others looked to follow Blow's success.

Big companies were paying attention too.

Over the next few years, consoles became

more open to indie games. The popularity

of gaming would create many opportunities

in gig work in the years to come.

CHAPTER TWO

WORKING A GIG JOB IN GAMING

In 2020, more than 3 billion people played video games. For those who want to turn a gaming pastime into money, there are plenty of opportunities. People can create their own games to sell online. Or they can work on parts of games made by others. Game companies hire people

Many gamers are able to turn their passion into gigs.

for short-term positions. Streamers can get

paid through subscribers and **sponsors**.

Freelance writers have plenty of places to

send stories about gaming.

MAKING THE GAME

There are many kinds of games. There are puzzles, murder mysteries, shooting games, and more. Games can run on many different devices. People play on computers, phones, and home consoles.

Every game starts with an idea. To make the idea into a game people can play, a developer must make choices. The developer must decide how to program the game. Many different programming languages are available. Simple games may be easier to program. Complicated ones might require advanced skills.

Game developers create a video game's code. This code determines how the game looks, how characters move, or how items work.

Several platforms give developers a way to sell games. Steam is popular, with more than 100 million users. A percentage of each sale goes to Steam. The Epic Games Store is another platform that works similarly.

Developers don't have to create games alone. They can find gigs with other

Some gig workers prefer to work alone or with indie companies. Other workers prefer working with larger companies.

indie developers or with big companies.

A freelancer can reach out to someone

who might need help on a project. Video

game artist and gig worker Daniel Rose

has worked with several different gaming

companies. He writes, "They must be

convinced through my art work and my professionalism that I am someone they want to work with."[4] Professionalism is behavior expected of a capable and qualified worker.

Games use many different sounds to help the play come to life. Musicians can get gigs making game music. Musicians may submit examples of their songs to the game maker. Voice actors can get gigs voicing game characters. To try out, actors might record examples of them acting. Or they might read lines given to them by the game maker.

Voice actors give video game characters their speaking voices. Many voice actors have their own recording software.

For some gigs, people might go to a studio to record sounds. People can record sounds at home too. They might need their own recording gear and instruments. They may need computers and **software** to prepare the audio for the game.

PLAYING THE GAME

Many people love to play games. Many others also love to watch games being played. Streamers take advantage of these two facts.

To start, streamers need a computer, a console, or a phone to play on. They need to choose a game to stream. They need devices or software to record and stream sound and video. Fairly cheap gear can get the job done. But better equipment can mean a better show. Streamers can use advanced software to add visual effects to their streams. This can add excitement for viewers.

Finally, a streamer needs to make an account on a streaming platform. There are many platforms available. They include Twitch, YouTube, Facebook Gaming, and others.

When a person creates content to stream, there are many approaches she can take. The streamer can play a game from beginning to end. She can aim to beat a record. Or she can entertain viewers in other ways while playing. A streamer might crack jokes or chat online with fans. The

streamer might review the game itself.

A streaming gig can make money

in multiple ways. For example, viewers

can watch a channel on Twitch for free.

But many fans subscribe to their favorite

VIRTUAL MUSIC SHOWS

Many performers play live music over the internet. A few have discovered a different gig. They create live shows within a video game. Bands such as 100 gecs and Massive Attack have played among the blocky streets and buildings of *Minecraft*. Rapper Travis Scott performed a game-stopping number in *Fortnite* in 2020. Live music events give gamers a chance to experience the energy of an in-person show without having to leave home.

TYLER "NINJA" BLEVINS

Some streamers make a little money. Others make a fortune. Tyler Blevins is a famous gamer known as Ninja. Ninja was the most followed gamer in 2019 with millions of fans. He's also earned millions. In fact, he made around $1 million for playing a game called *Apex Legends* on the day it came out. Ninja has kept his viewers with his energy, skills, and willingness to stream for hours a day.

channel. They support the streamer by paying him money regularly. Subscribers can get benefits like being able to post in special chats. Fans can also get more rewards by paying more. Fans give one-time payments as tips. Streamers also get paid from the ads a platform runs on their channel.

Sponsors are another source of money. Streamers can connect with a gaming company in order to advertise the company's products. This is called becoming an affiliate of the company. The gamer can post affiliate ads on his or her channel. If viewers click on those links and go to the company's website to buy the product, the streamer gets paid part of the price. For example, a streamer on Twitch can have an ad that's selling the game she's playing at that moment.

WRITING ABOUT THE GAMES

There are many places for video game journalists to sell their words. Many websites and magazines focus on video games. They often use freelancers to create content. But a freelance writer must prove he's the best person to write the story.

Editor Drew Sleep suggested new game journalists first get started with a **blog**. "You must have experience [with] writing, because writing is going to be quite a lot of your job," he said.[5]

Writers set up their blogs and try to make them look appealing. They can post about

The Electronic Entertainment Expo, or E3, is an event where many video game companies announce upcoming projects. Many journalists go there to write about new games or consoles.

whatever gaming topics interest them. A

blog can help a journalist learn how she

wants to write and what she wants to

write about. Through blogging, writers can

start to connect with others in the field.

The blogger may hear news about a new

game coming out that she can spread to her readers. Like a streaming channel, a popular blog can have sponsors and affiliate ads.

To get a gig with a magazine or website, the writer approaches an editor. An editor is the person in charge of the written content that gets published. The freelancer pitches an idea. Editors need all sorts of writing. Along with big articles, there are often smaller news pieces. Websites might need someone to write scripts for videos. Editors can also reach out to writers the editor has worked with in the past with an idea.

Video game reporters need to be aware of trends in video games. This means playing games and going to video game events regularly.

Once a writer gets the gig, he must write the story. He might talk to an interesting developer and write an article about the developer. The writer might play a game so he can review it. Even when not writing, a journalist can go to gaming events and keep up with gaming news.

CHAPTER THREE

PROS AND CONS OF GIG JOBS IN GAMING

Some workers have another job and take gigs on the side. Others make a living just through gigs. Some people enjoy the freedom of gaming gigs. Others have no choice. They work a gaming gig because it's all a company has offered them. Every kind of gig job has its pros and cons.

Some gig workers at video game studios want permanent positions. However, full-time jobs aren't always available.

THE PROS

A lot of gamers are already committed to

the world of gaming. Gig work offers people

the promise of doing what they love and

making a living. For example, streamers can build a fun community online. Journalists work with others who also are excited about gaming.

Even people who want a full-time job may start with a gig at a company. The work helps them gain experience. The company may end up hiring them for a more stable position. It can be very hard to make the switch from a gig to permanent work. But some people value the opportunity.

There's often something new to do with each gig. A developer might get the chance to work on several different kinds of games.

Some independent contractors learn new skills working for a game studio. However, they don't always get paid more for new responsibilities.

Gig workers might gain new skills on the

job. For example, one worker took a gig

at a small game company. She was only

supposed to be writing a story for a game.

But her tasks quickly grew. She said, "I did

everything under the sun including work in Unreal [a game engine], sound design, systems design, combat design, writing, playtesting . . . you name it."[6]

Some gig workers can choose where and when to work. A gig worker might work from home. A journalist might travel to places to meet people to write about. Workers might move to a whole new area to work a gig for a company.

Some gig workers have opportunities to try out free products. Journalists sometimes get new games so they can write an early review. Some game publishers even pay

Many players rely on journalists to review games before buying them.

popular streamers to play a new game. It's

a good deal for everyone. The streamer's

followers see the game in action. Or people

get to read the inside scoop ahead of time.

Viewers and readers might be inspired

Many independent contractors are hired for a few months at a time. They have to find other work when the contract is up.

to buy their own copy of the game.

The company gets the chance to make

more sales.

THE CONS

It can be hard to break into gig work

in gaming. A lot of the work is unpaid.

For example, thousands of streamers make gaming content online. It can be hard for a streamer to find viewers. A streamer needs to keep playing even without a fan base. It may take a long time for people to discover the streamer.

Low numbers of viewers make it harder to make money. Fewer people are available to support or tip the streamer. Ad money is tied to the number of people seeing those ads. And companies want to make affiliate deals with the most popular gamers.

Journalists can work hard creating an article idea only for it not to be published.

Good developers put a lot of work into games. But their project competes with all the other games out there. Steam alone offers tens of thousands of games.

Once someone is making money, the pay can be low. Brett Helling owns a website about gig jobs. In a piece on game journalism, he wrote, "It takes time to find stable, high-paying work."[7] A developer doesn't know if a game will make much money. Streamers can't count on tips. Magazines and websites that a freelancer writes for can go out of business. That makes it hard to plan one's life.

Some people who work with a short-term contract at a larger company don't want a gig. They would like the company to hire them full-time. But the company saves

Without vacation or sick days, some workers feel pressure to go to work when they are ill. If they don't work that day, they don't get paid.

money by using gig workers. Unlike full-time

workers, gig workers don't have many

benefits. For example, the company doesn't

give them paid sick days or vacations.

Specific gigs can have specific

challenges. For example, many games

require voice actors to scream. Screaming

over and over again can hurt someone's voice. The actor may have to take a long break to recover. Sometimes an actor can cause lasting harm to her voice.

STANDING OUT FROM THE CROWD

There are many things someone can do to improve his chances for gig jobs. If he is a developer, he can take classes to build his skills. Streamers can practice playing. Journalists can take courses to learn more about gaming or about writing.

A streamer can consider which platforms work best for her needs. A popular platform is full of viewers. But well-used platforms are already packed full of streamers. A new channel has a harder time getting noticed. On the other hand, a less popular platform has fewer viewers but also fewer streamers competing for fans.

LIFE ON STREAM

On March 14, 2021, popular streamer Ludwig Ahgren started a new video. He told his viewers that for every new subscriber, he'd keep going another ten seconds. As tens of thousands of people signed up, Ahgren kept his promise. Sometimes he gamed. Sometimes he hung out with people. He hosted movie nights. Fans even chatted with each other while he slept on-screen. After thirty-one days, the stream finally ended. Ahgren took a well-earned break.

To bring in both viewers and sponsors, streamers can make their channels appear more appealing. They might include fun pictures. They can organize their information so it's easier to read. Also, viewers enjoy more than just watching the games. Many streamers chat while they play. Streamers might be funny. They might have a point of view to share. All of these things can keep people tuning in. Sometimes a streamer puts on a special event to gain viewers.

CHAPTER FOUR

THE FUTURE OF GIG JOBS IN GAMING

The video game business keeps growing. It shows no signs of stopping as more and more people begin playing games every year. With all the money coming in, the opportunities for gig jobs will probably increase. But the nature of gig jobs could change, too. For example,

Cyberpunk 2077 was a game released in 2020. It was controversial because of how many issues the game had when it came out.

governments and companies are arguing over who counts as a gig worker.

INDIES OF THE FUTURE

The game market has only grown more and more crowded. Even big companies can't count on guaranteed sales. The huge costs involved in creating games make each new project a risk. For example, the studio CD Projekt Red spent more than $300 million on a game called *Cyberpunk 2077*. But when *Cyberpunk 2077* came out in 2020, it was packed full of problems. Many unhappy buyers returned the game. *Cyberpunk 2077* still made money. But it was less than the studio expected.

Independent developers usually spend much less when making games. Losing money is bad for an indie, but it won't lead to ruin. However, the ease with which anyone can put out a game is adding to the

market overload.

A single developer can build something

popular in a few months as long as the idea

is appealing. But the game doesn't have to

UNREAL ENGINE 5

In 2021, the company Epic Games presented an early version of its latest game development software, Unreal Engine 5. Developers had used earlier Unreal Engines for 3D graphics in popular games like *Fortnite*. Unreal Engine 5 made scenes look even more real. Lighting became more natural. Environments and objects could look more detailed. Games would run more smoothly even with incredible graphics.

be simple. The latest versions of software such as Unreal Engine let developers do more and more difficult things without worrying about complex coding. Developer Sofi Naydenova said, "The border between indie and big games will blur, as the technology is developing and there are more possibilities for a small studio to make a really cool game."[8]

One of the most popular indie games has been *Stardew Valley*. It was not made over a weekend. For more than four years, Eric Barone worked all week long, twelve hours a day. He did every part himself, designing

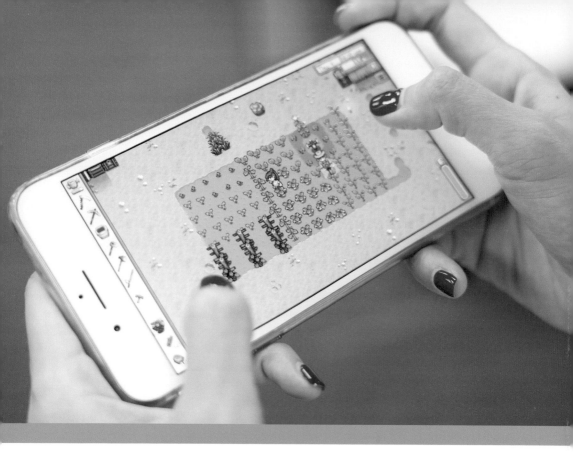

Stardew Valley *is a popular farming game. Many players turned to the calming game during the COVID-19 pandemic.*

and programming everything. He had

taught himself to code. In *Stardew Valley*,

the player takes over a run-down farm. The

player also helps people in town. Barone

gave the villagers unique characteristics

and stories. He spent a long time perfecting the artwork. He even wrote and made the game music by himself. Finally, the game was published. People loved it. *Stardew Valley* sold millions of copies. All of Barone's hard work had paid off.

THE FURTHER RISE OF STREAMING

In 2020, the COVID-19 pandemic hit the world. Governments asked people to avoid travel to stop the spread of the dangerous disease. People stayed home. They couldn't go out or get together with friends. So people spent more time online. Many watched livestreams. The streamed

THE GROWTH OF TWITCH

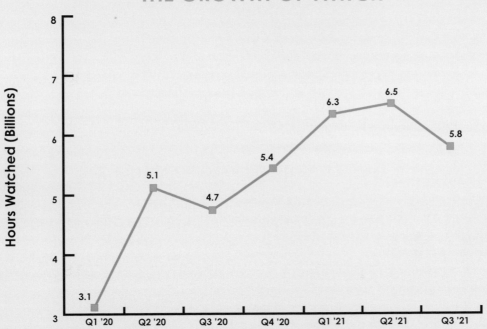

Hours Watched (Billions)

8 —
7 —
6 —
5 —
4 —
3 —

3.1 — Q1 '20
5.1 — Q2 '20
4.7 — Q3 '20
5.4 — Q4 '20
6.3 — Q1 '21
6.5 — Q2 '21
5.8 — Q3 '21

Source: Ethan May, "Streamlabs and Stream Hatchet Q3 2021 Live Streaming Industry Report," Streamlabs, October 27, 2021. https://streamlabs.com.

After the start of the COVID-19 pandemic, people spent more and more time watching streamers on platforms like Twitch.

content included music performances and exercise classes.

Plenty of the content focused on gaming. In 2020, viewers watched 100 billion hours of game streaming on YouTube alone.

And more viewers meant more companies were interested in becoming sponsors or in running ads. The situation with COVID-19 changed over time. Governments began allowing more travel, but the growth in streaming did not slow. For example, viewers watched 45 percent more hours on Twitch in 2021 than in 2020.

Another trend in game streaming is the entrance of e-sports. E-sports stands for electronic sports. In e-sports, people compete by playing video games either as individuals or as parts of teams. Players can get salaries. Each match has prize money,

E-sports teams work together to beat other teams. Fortnite, League of Legends, and Overwatch are all popular e-sports games.

and sponsors offer support. However,

e-sports aren't for the casual gamer. Players

practice long hours just to gain enough

skills to make it onto a team.

Once on a team, players may practice

their game for ten hours or more a day.

Winning takes huge amounts of effort and

skill. Lucas "Mendo" Håkansson started out

playing the game *Overwatch*. *Overwatch*

is a shooting game. Two teams face off

against each other.

E-SPORTS

Video game competitions were not widely known when they started in the 1970s. By 2020, the competitions, known as e-sports, had become big business. That year, about 439 million people watched e-sports events. Contests happened around the world. Colleges have e-sports programs, and college students have their own chances to compete. Individual games have their own leagues and world cups. E-sports are expected to keep growing in the future.

Similar to other e-sports gamers, Håkansson spent his practice time alone in a tiny room without windows. He worried about losing his edge if *Overwatch* ever changed its characters. He said, "It was honestly a miserable experience being there."[9] He left his e-sports team soon after joining. Players like Håkansson switch to streaming to escape the pressure. They want the control over their own work that a gig job offers.

Some streamers are going in the opposite direction and being picked up by teams. Håkansson himself was signed by another club right after he began streaming. Streamers might start to compete as well as streaming, or they might just stream. Teams can help a streamer make business plans and find sponsors. Some teams give the streamer a salary. In return, having a popular streamer on a team can pull in a lot of attention and money.

WHO COUNTS AS A GIG WORKER?

Companies save a lot of money by hiring gig workers. The companies don't have to pay the workers benefits such as sick leave. Some gig workers work alongside regular workers. They do almost the same

Gig work in gaming offers many workers flexibility. However, this flexibility can come at a cost.

job. Companies must do certain things to

make sure these people still qualify as gig

workers. Sometimes the company makes

them wear identification. But sometimes

the difference between the two kinds of

workers isn't very clear. Governments are considering who gig workers are and how companies should treat them.

In the future, gaming companies may hire fewer people as gig workers. Gig workers in gaming may form unions. Unions are organizations made up of members who do similar kinds of work. They can push businesses to make changes. Unions can win better wages and other benefits for gig workers. Only time will show how all of these things affect the future of gig jobs.

Many gig workers work on multiple projects at the same time. This allows them to make more money.

GLOSSARY

blog

a website meant for posting regular writings

developers

people who create something, such as games

freelancer

a person who works for different companies and gets paid for each project

gig

a temporary job

platform

a company or service that hosts content

software

computer programs that do specific tasks

sponsors

people or companies that provide money or other support

subscribe

to sign up to get something regularly, either for free or by paying money on a regular basis

SOURCE NOTES

INTRODUCTION: STREAMING A RECORD

1. Niftski, "Super Mario Bros. Any% Speedrun in 4:54:948 *FWR*" *YouTube*, April 7, 2021. www.youtube.com.

CHAPTER ONE: THE HISTORY OF GIG JOBS IN GAMING

2. Quoted in Chris Baker, "Stewart Brand Recalls First 'Spacewar' Tournament," *Rolling Stone*, May 25, 2016. www.rollingstone.com.

3. Quoted in Tracey Lien, "How Indie Games Went Mainstream," *Polygon*, October 4, 2013. www.polygon.com.

CHAPTER TWO: WORKING A GIG JOB IN GAMING

4. Daniel Rose, "A Video Game Artist's Guide to the Gig Economy," *Medium*, October 31, 2018. https://medium.com.

5. Quoted in Caroline Scott, "Key Advice for Getting Started in Games Journalism," *Jouralism.co.uk*, October 14, 2015. www.journalism.co.uk.

CHAPTER THREE: PROS AND CONS OF GIG JOBS IN GAMING

6. Quoted in Colin Campbell, "The Game Industry's Disposable Workers," *Polygon*, December 16, 2019. www.polygon.com.

7. Brett Helling, "A Complete Guide to Video Game Journalism Jobs," *Gigworker*, February 4, 2020. https://gigworker.com.

CHAPTER FOUR: THE FUTURE OF GIG JOBS IN GAMING

8: Quoted in Harry Cole, "What's the Future for Indie Games?" *Ind13 Games*, June 5, 2020. www.ind13.com.

9. Quoted in Cecilia D'Anastasio, "Gaming Influencers Are the Future of Esports," *Wired*, May 13, 2021. www.wired.com.

FOR FURTHER RESEARCH

BOOKS

Heidi Ayarbe, *Gig Jobs in High-Tech*. San Diego, CA: BrightPoint Press, 2023.

Josh Gregory, *PC Gaming: Beginner's Guide*. Ann Arbor, MI: Cherry Lake Publishing, 2022.

Joshua Romphf, *Coding Activities for Developing Games in Unity*. New York: Rosen Publishing Group, 2022.

INTERNET SOURCES

Brett Helling, "A Complete Guide to Video Game Journalism Jobs," *Gigworker*, January 31, 2021. www.gigworker.com.

"How to Become a Coder: Pauline's Story," *BBC Bitesize*, n.d. www.bbc.co.uk/bitesize.

Keith Stuart, "15 Video Game Streamers Your Teens Should Be Watching," *Guardian*, March 15, 2021. www.theguardian.com.

WEBSITES

Code.org
www.code.org

Code.org is a website offering resources and classes for students to learn about coding.

Gaming Careers
https://gamingcareers.com

Gaming Careers is a website that has articles on livestreaming games and how to improve streams.

Scratch
https://scratch.mit.edu

Scratch is a website that allows kids and teens to code their own programs, including games. The website features an online community with a team that monitors community content.

INDEX

IMAGE CREDITS

ABOUT THE AUTHOR

Clara MacCarald is a freelance writer with a master's degree in ecology and natural resources. She lives with her family in an off-grid house nestled in the forests of central New York. When not parenting her daughter, she spends her time writing nonfiction books for kids.